NEW POEMS

NEW POEMS

Joshua Krugman

DEERFIELD ACADEMY PRESS

DEERFIELD

DEERFIELD ACADEMY PRESS

7 BOYDEN LANE

DEERFIELD, MASSACHUSETTS 01342

ISBN : 0-9755758-7-2

PRINTED IN THE UNITED STATES OF AMERICA

me & the zeitgeist 2/15/08

MANIFESTO

Poetry in the twentyfirst century transcends traditional poetic meaning. It lives in its own dimension, free of any concepts or precepts but its own. It conforms to nothing, supplies nothing, lacks nothing, asks nothing. It is a dispassionate observatory into the world from without, and out of the human mind from within. It is disassociated from all cultural and municipal laws except for the most basic lingual conventions necessary to convey it. Poems in the twentyfirst century move beyond and disassemble all traditional conceptual associations tied to love, hate, fear, anguish, despair, elation, irony, sincerity, worship, linear rationality. The relations between the poems form their own associative framework. Conventional sentimental significance was dead after the First World War, and we're still trying to kill it. The world has no meaning except that which humans choose to assign to it. These poems assign to the world no meaning. The twentyfirst century poet writes about the existence of material and immaterial things and the lack of existence of material and immaterial things as the poet sees them or wishes to see them. Twentyfirst century poets have freed themselves from the fetters of morality, politics, sexuality, metaphor, biology, obscenity, inadequacy, creation and   destruction, fullness and emptiness, individuality and collectivism, violence and kindness, tonality and atonality, materiality and immateriality, majority and minority, all dualism, humanity, the understanding of humanity, nature, the understanding of nature, power, concepts of power, property and theft, language, personality, equality, all immediate time, statistical tendency, labour, currency, all things that can and cannot be seen, heard, understood, felt, smelled, expected, tasted, coveted, balanced, influenced, imagined, loved, worshipped, abhorred. The modern poet dispenses with everything dispensable, until only the poem remains. The modern poet hurls the poem at nothingness and if it returns to the poet, it is a good poem. The twentyfirst century poet works in simultaneity rather than exclusivism, and the metaphors the poet employs differentiate as well as liken. Rather than evoking emotions (meaning) directly, poetry in the twentyfirst century induces, in its reader, the experience of the memory of meaning.

by the time
sweet sue was out the door
fifty someodd fireflies
had filtered through the floor,
and the whisper of something missing,
something more—
emanated unendingly from
cigarette-smolders of paper men—
told something held in store.

they battle with vagrant saxophones
(these embers of humanity
clinging to the mustard street).
their striations of slack muscle
tease and squeeze the last ironic bar
of night's strange symphony,
then go silent.

—and the ones and twos of morning
begin their parade around the park.

rollerskating
across vinyl sidewalks
hollering hallelujah, hanging
calamity on a nail
by the door.

> street lights are car keys,
> people are bees,
> coffeestained napkins float
> like diseased moths —

no, it's better this way
and crisscrossed
like frayed fabric
or the wakes of aeroplanes:
little holes in
our little sky.

> people are trees,
> trees are leaves,
> everyone leaves
> and the firebombs come.
> people are watching it
> on television.

a boat bobs on the daffodil sea.
sealions
bark, dismembered violins speak in
postcards, and the sun always
sets in a bowl.

thoughts from a meadow in mid-may

3

so many puddles, and you can't see them all
because so many teagreen seagreen dandelioned
tussocks of newgrass grassgreen grass hide
the puddles between and beneath themselves.

so many: some, any. shards of grass are estuaries
of puddles: an amazed maze. squelch, squelch.

4

when your fingers get too cold,
you can always talk to me, you know,
and i'll remember everything you say.
you told me about
when your brother killed his beloved goat
because you lived in india then
and one-had-to-do-these-things.
and i told you about my hummingbird
whose eyes were polished peppercorns
and you said if i cried, my eyes would be
just two rusty pennies.

8

a bobolink nest in the field:
—a bobbing bobbin
weaving loose on the interwoven
ungleaned hay, haplessly strewn.

12

i remember my baptism
in the wings of the moth you gave me.
it died in the cold bathroom
where it was in a jar to keep safe
til morning.

13

i haven't seen anyone stabbed:
i don't live in the city
and i've stopped watching those movies.

you fell instantly in love with
the stabbed boy
—his jaw etched slightly
the edges of unformulated expression—
and you attended the
breaths in his stainedglass cheeks.

22

to reside in the mind of michelangelo
and slide through understanding thick fingers
into the world.
to safely lie in colorless formless unrealized syllables,
and fall asleep in sculpture.

a storm:
trees' ragged appendages
strewn across the road.

strolling through the wreck, i imagine
a bemused vireo looking for her eggs
among striped acorns and lastyear leaves.
the threads of her nest became
feathers in the flank of the wind.

cleaning agents
alone in the closet:
can they hear
sounds of feet
alone on the corridor's
indestructible floor?

darkness is a hard nut
to crack, you say
while finger-painting
the contours of empty leaves.

quite alone, a dead canary
is flopped on the sidewalk,
slanting like a louisiana vowel
under the flowerboxes
and leaded-glass windows
of the roomy apartment up there.

you wonder, why haven't they
changed the glass? what if a child ate it?
and
        how did the canary die?

dropping
        pebbles in
              to
              a

              (
)
              (

              p u d d l e

to—
        (to see)
            s e e—
                to look at how—
(perhaps)
                     if

              m   i   r r o r e   d

. . . again
and   again
       and
again

the pebbles would cease to be
any
  more

or
less

m e a n i n g f u l

than   *y|o|u|*

                                   —or far away.

a white moth fluttered around
the big wooden rafters
above the schumann string quartet:
flourwhite torso bebopping and bobbing
on the swirling thermals of music:
conducting, with chalky wings,
the ferocious scherzo below.

counting the day in minutes,
a second in hours;
counting the tiles in the bathtub
(and the half-tiles too),
then lying on the old floral sofa
like a fillet of day-old fish—
waiting, waiting for someone
to touch your shoulderblade
with a heavy palm and say,
come upstairs, come through the skylight,
or: there's just a chance of rain
so we might as well swim
before we go.

For a long time I waited,
following the seams in the carpet.
I knew that we would be old,
and have to guide our dreams
to make them converge.
You tell me you picture yourself
as old as the tattered carpet.
Dawn dawns, and the next dream
is of something entirely different.

Shostakovich sq#1 Cmt#1
Sept 15 —

it's raining hard.

.falling
.in
.the
.water;

        i press my forehead
                up against the cold windowpane

.falling
.on
.the
.ground;

        the glass singes my syncopated thoughts.

.falling
.through
.the
.trees:

rain muddies the lake
and makes the earth shiny and paradisiacal.

and snow. And
.wind.
yes.
after a while was over
and the thin crackle of ice on
the pond had thickened...

the white prayer of frost in
              your eyes
hypnotizes me.

.and then it
              happened.

tick tick tick, and the squirrels
              buried us in our shells
—under the hands of austere treebranches—
delicate.

it's only the sideaffects, dear.
fall into my arms and rock and roll baby.

hemlocks

hemlock trees unhinge in high winds.
as kids, my brother and i
pictured we were strong enough
to brace their corrugated trunks
and save them with our arms.

hemlocks always break
about twelve feet above the ground—
sometimes the spire clings by twisted bark
to survive diagonally.

normally, rivers
diverge unquestioned,
untaxed, carrying
their deephearted lives
in their stomachs.

from above,
rivers are not rivers
but thoughts
fragile as hair—
limp and taut
across the land and land.

if everything were assigned a color,
showing my brother how to do chin-ups
on the reverse side of the staircase
and imitating the laugh of my dad's lover
would be—an incandescent cerulean.

youth left my eyes
in a single tear
at the age of five,
and i didn't tell my mother about it
until i ran full-tilt into the
refrigerator eight years later.
this is, and you can disagree,
pulsating magenta
struck with lung-orange.

such remembrances are like seeing
the incurable blue agony of sunset
reflected in the long striations
of the dark lake's dying bouquet,
and not being able to suppress
the onset of a light and lonely sleep.

after a crucifixion

the tide ebbed,
the grass grew back on the mountain.

the children lifted frogs
by the legs from the stream,
and there wasn't even a tea-stain tan
on their shoulders.

outside there's air,
there's trees waving
tentacles, trees waving
out where there's air
waving trees out there
waving hair waving
eyelashes of small and broken
grasses under trees,
high as the sky and low
as a low voice. low as
a lover's low voice
lonely in the refulgent
bassoon-damp air of
evening outside there's
evening there's evening
outside there's evening
eventhough evening is
gone there's trees waving
wavers, paper crowns,
paper gowns going down
like a lover's low voice,
like a low voice,
like a tall waving eyelash
waving tree waving
wavering evening outside
on the waves, on the evening
out there there's not a care,
not an eyelash of a care
out there there's enough

evening trees waving
tentacles, shoelaces, low voices,
wavering eye lashes
low broken grasses,
eventhough evening is gone.

two minutes til the end of time,
five dollars and sixty cents for birdseed,
three-point longshot ends the game,
four plates at supper (minus my brother plus you).
there's no more
bread in the box
salt in the lox
chickens in the pox
or feet in the socks.
speaking of doc,
the sheriff's pimply thugs went up the hill
and burnt stalin's effigy
the other night—
taught him a lesson.
they said it appeased
mother earth.

    ok, i get it, so it's not stylish
    to be beautiful anymore:
    you have to know
    the physics of the nuclear bullet
    to get a government job.
    but i'm not frankly concerned
    with that.
    i'd rather stare at nothing
    till it turns purple and then go inside
    the microwave to see if
    i can see the waves.
    there was always plenty of seaglass—

the torture of the sea
made it smooth.

life is whittling me
down to a toothpick and it hurts,
but at least the boyscouts are taking new
recruits. you'd better sign up too.
they give you a free application
to the marines when you graduate.

the streetsigns say one mile til the next rest-stop,
four minutes til bedtime,
seventeen trillion national dept.
the fire department has six engines, five hoses,
and several interns who can't count.

Long before getting lost with my kazoo in the Kalahari

anyway, i'll tell you about it if you want.
there's not much to hear,
so to make it interesting i'll start in the middle
and tell it to both ends at once.
and when that's done and gone,
like armistice day,
the bread will still be moldy in the breadbox
and the books strewn about the floor.
but it's no matter to tidy up the garage at least—
my mother practically lived there
before she moved away.

if you get hungry,
there's wine in the suitcases
and the stove works just fine,
except on sunday evenings
when the Parsons hog all the electricity,
cranking up the airconditioner so loud
you can hear it in Mission County.

silhouette

he's a man, a nearby city, a block of ice.
his mistress is two thirds of everything
and half of what's left.

look at him—hobbling like faulkner in a jar.
he can't put his socks on.
he's a bookworm without eyes,
farming his mind out to political marionettes.

—

he and karl marx took coffee together in yugoslavia
way back when,
and since then he paints his eyebrows on
and wears stolen cowboy boots.

his mother was a dancer in a bar.
she reads roald dahl like warm beer in the afternoon—
she's his darling Andromeda.
he was her Persephone
when they drove through the outskirts
singing mosaics of janis joplin and claude debussy.

—

he's a spindly umbrella
in a broken laundry machine,
a pulse in my cracked terracotta bowl.

he's leaning out of his window now,
looking across the empty courtyard, crying.

but it's not as bad as all that.
the mail still comes to the mailbox
and the ants pilgrimage
to the sugar. the preacher
still visits to listen to La Bohème
and asks me is everything all right
and i say, nothing hot soup can't fix.

yes, i tell him,
i'm quite well: in fact, when Charlemagne
came over for tea the other day,
he told me, rusty helmet in hand,
a body needs sleep, no matter
how many peonies one plants.
in parting he said, women dig a conquistador.
that's interesting, i replied.

sojourning

prerequisite palmoil palpitations,
permutations of culminating perspirations,
pile into VW bugs like misplaced aspirations—
and sentimental equations look on,
displeased, while under quaking leaves,
in long lived-in rubber sleeves,
lie limply dreamy sheaves
(under the quaking leaves),
where discontinuous disenfranchised
disloyal dystopian dyslexic
trigonometric dialectic diadems
deem other jewelry unworthy
of swarthy swaths of swanlike stems
of pumpernickel pumpkinseed
pallid-faced perfunctoriness,
passing on other playthings
to communistic dandelion rings
where the solitary lilac sings,
prone to myriad nostalgical wanderings
through cloudy cartesian springs
springing with lingering fingerling
ding-dong bells, ping-pong balls
from which fall hypnotic hypersensitive
trembling remembering hippie hopi
hallucinogenic methods of coping,
and then, walking alone across the sloping

painted desert, deserted, feet hurted,
and not moping, moseying with the sky lightly flirted,
eyelids skirted with inert desserts,
and all at once, looking askance,
begin to dancing prance,
blowing on the cheeks of chance,
and remember a refrain of refracted
reasoning, well-rooted in the teeth of time,
well-tied to the trunk of the truck-thick tree,
tremulous with triumphant tempests,
tempting the torpid tented entrails
to invert their shoestrings and so invent
a maneuver so malleable it could untie
the strongest heartstrings
and bowstrings, dissected thought-streams,
strung from nowhere to nowhere on the nowhere express
(dressed for stress, stressed for dress,
riding on the nowhere express),
and it's a long way home for sure.
surely looking so demure,
no one'll endure long enough to take the cure,
and die with dismal dimples and permanent curls
curling in long flourishing swirls
into the vandalized vanishing points
of vainly vaccinated imagination,
devolving with exquisite sad dervishes
of unutterable eye-cancers.

.

microwave

It seems that
all color
has slid off the edge of the spoon
leaving only the residue of its reflection
across the room,
where rubberbands and duct-tape
hold the refrigerator together
and the microwave is melting
your children.

someone gave you a microwave.
they thought you were stone-age enough
not to have one yet.

the microwave wasn't
a state-of-the-art contraption—
it was an old jalopy several feet wide
like an obese square rodent.

they said, if you don't want it,
feel free to give it to the Survival Center:
they'll be glad to have it.

but right now it's sitting lopsided
on a pretty wicker chair in your kitchen,
awaiting judgment.
you can't hurry progress.

space monkey

a monkey's lips
kiss the planet
in the window
of a small dismal idea
falling thousands of miles an hour
without any fuel.

he's another hot mystery
whizzing like a
revolver carousel:
plastic gravity adhering to
dead simian lips.

"up on the roof..."
  -Laura Nyro singing an old Motown tune.

up on the roof
baby up on the roof,
watching the grass crawl
black into the river.
up on the roof,
tall as the trees almost,
we're a sailboat asleep
up on the roof
we're a rumor
on the sea, on the black grass
crawling hyperextended
in the river between
the cheeks of the mountains,
true for themselves,
a rumor in the river
up on the roof
baby up on the roof
we've got blankets for skin
and stars for eyes.
on the roof we've got
airplane hair and starry
eyes: bells in the morning
up on the roof
a red star—a wheelbarrow.
a red star—a living thing.

up on the roof baby,
up there on the roof
there's plenty to see,
and plenty to be
up on the roof.

i. the funeral—

wait a minute while we get reacquainted
with the body—and clothing.
once we're all gathered and
nothing no-longer perturbs us,
we can stare at the floor
while the ceiling swirls above.

seagulls swing also,
sealing the ceiling shut with sealing-wax
and stealing the unassuming swallow-flight
of achingly unimportant urchin-shells,
bastioning at the bottom of the sea
and always settling further into sleep,
though they seemingly stir not.

ii. the eulogy—

maurice's hair was always
perfect,
but no one mentioned that
for fear of sounding
—impolite.
instead they sputtered about
those he "left behind."

maurice also loved michelangelo,
but no one knew that
except maurice (and michelangelo),
depending.

on how precisely a viennese waltz
is transformed by a thick carpet

cloaked figures
stand around
moaning on cigarettes
and swimming
into the abyss,
then throwing their shoes
over telephone lines.

anyone who misses
the train to chiapas
sleeps on the platform
until daylight
and watches the
staccato starlings
try to eat the dew
off the sidewalk.

tragic observations from early autumn

we should set the sky on fire
sometime
so the earth glows
like a huge lantern
hanging orangely in nowhereness
to show people the way.

i found the lupines
you pressed in *The Brothers Karamazov*.
i love you with so much of myself
that none of me is left
to do the dishes.

*

the rain whispers like knives
on sheaves of dewfilled grass
asleep—
not knowing whether today
is already tomorrow.

*

the clouds burned and wafted
as the moon rose—a rose).

watching it frantically,
trees and winedark water
rendered it again.
telescopically far away
were people.

*

The snake has an egg in its long body:
Its thin child is curled there.

*

Ants gather at the knife
on the faux-granite counter.
The blade is wet with
disemboweling a fruit.
Using the knife, you can
squash the ants easily.

*

take me there on dahlias' asphodel
skiff. your voice is new,
and we are wise and young

among the sapling trees
your starfish hands handle my cheeks.

*

what would a poppy say
if it could talk? would it talk?
would this popping jalopy poppy drop
its pendulous petals in ecstasy
or would it shrug
to face the sun
instead?

professors sit with their feet on mahogany desks,
thinking about "the karma of divorce"
(in the broadest sense), and fall asleep
with books on their stomachs,
while outside their offices
unpostulated repercussions form fishing nets
in the everywhere ocean of emoting ideas.
fish eat these glinting gestures
and come to life to teach the sky
to love its wide-eyed vigil.

last night

meryl streep and alexander
(the great), came over for dinner
last night with a kosher steak.
the sun was rising and the tide was low
so we all decided to go for a row.
the scissors were eating the sky
and the Surprise was nigh
so we decided to laugh rather than cry.
dystrophy is inevitable—
love it. feel its arthritic
cognition caress your
osteoporotic soul and squeeze you
like an orange—but so lovingly!
and it almost doesn't hurt.
you shouldn't have bought
so many rubberbands.
it'll be hopeless to untangle the moon.
when she got wind of Starvation,
she shook her fist (which was, of course, pluto),
and then they said it wasn't a planet
in retaliation,
and she cried for six months
and then got really smashed
with bob dylan and plato,
and bangladesh flooded again with her
tears, but no one heard about it

because it wasn't on CNN
and therefore it didn't happen.
meanwhile, over supper,
several bloodhounds
and a loony cocker-spaniel
were discussing the calculus of pencil shavings
and saying how there were
people-shapes in the clouds,
laughing so hard they wet the carpet.
god knows why, but it was kind of
a bluesy night, so the streetlights
were more butter-yellow than usual
and the spoons wouldn't lie flat
in their drawer. footsteps were syncopated
and the washing machine
sounded like a washboard
with an ax to grind
and that's not just a figure of speech.
if you're goin' to argentina,
tell all the people i'm a-comin' too.
not only am i coming,
but i'm bringin' betty sue.

a train out of town

let's jump a minute
to where the tall ticket guy
comes out from behind the pew,
and says, would you care for white tea,
and i say no, and he says,
do you have a ticket
and howabout you
and howabout you,
and i say, we were in a rush
but we'll sleep on the ceiling
and not take up any room.
and he says
fine,
fine,
right down the line,
and he hadn't been so happy
since pall mall changed wrappers in seventy-three,
but that's another story
(like thinking you can fly
and then flying),
and i called your name several times
before i woke you up,
but the house is burned now
and you'll never believe me.
the seats in the train
smell like new bluejeans

and whiteout, but kindof good
like gasoline is kindof good
if you're convinced it won't give you cancer.
everytime we went around a corner
we fell off the ceiling,
and at first it was fun,
and then it was a game,
and then somebody yelled
i found Jesus
i found Jesus
and that was good
because there was a magenta
missing person watch for him
and now he'd turned up,
but all we had to give him
was white tea,
and it was the dregs
so it had leaves in it
and he complained at first
but someone gave him a joint
and he didn't complain after that,
and you and i were velcroed
to the ceiling still
like a piece of hair on a balloon,
but i wasn't sure
if we were the balloon or the hair,
and i still wasn't sure if i was
dreaming anyway or not because you
hadn't talked in ten minutes,

and then you talked
but it was about arthropods
so i wasn't satisfied
but decided it was hopeless no matter what
and started drinking white tea again
and looking at the scenery.
the scenery was scenic:
trees and moss, moss and leaves
interwoven in an orgy of agedness,
and we were like water,
water in water on water
and much more at home this way,
and the trees were watching,
moving and unmoving at once.
in fact, everything was all at once.
our eyes didn't move together,
yours and mine
and mine and mine
and mine and yours
and yours and yours
and yours and our
eyes weren't moving together,
but the overall effect was
the ravens started coming in,
which wasn't surprising,
seeing as what kind of night it was
and what the trees
had been roaring on and on about till now.
and the ravens just rose and fell

with the slipstream
like they knew
there was either catastrophe
or utopian stoptime ecstasy
coming around the next ridge
and like any good mother,
they were gonna be there when
it happened.

BIOGRAPHY

Joshua Krugman has lived for seventeen years, most of which has happened between November twenty-eighth, 1990, and the present. He wrote these poems between May and November, 2007. He resides at the edge of a hemlock forest in Sunderland, Massachusetts with some of his close relatives. He tries not to be influenced by the work of T.S. Elliot, William Carlos Williams, William Butler Yeats, William Shakespeare, Mary Oliver, Allen Ginsberg, Patti Smith, E.E. Cummings, and Bob Dylan. He views these poems as consecutive and simultaneous thoughts, prayer beads, and root vegetables. They should be read in the order in which they appear.

*

MAY 2008
HALLOWELL'S PRINTING
GREENFIELD MASSACHUSETTS
*